Lifestream

Journey Into Past & Future Lives

Shelley Kaehr, Ph.D.

FIRST EDITION, 2003
Fifth Printing, 2005

Edited by Cheryl Doyle
Cover design by Shelley Kaehr

Library of Congress Control Number:
2003090056

Kaehr, Shelley A., 1967—
        Lifestream/
Shelley Kaehr—1ˢᵗ ed.
                p.   c.m.
                Includes bibliographical refer-
                ences.
                ISBN 0-9719340-3-7

If you wish to contact the author or would like
more information about this book, please
write to the author in care of An Out of This
World Production and we will forward your
request. Please write to:

Shelley Kaehr, Ph.D.
c/o An Out of This World Production
P.O. Box 610943
Dallas, TX 75261-0943

To JD
In Memory

Also by
Shelley Kaehr, Ph.D.

Books:

Origins of Huna: Secret Behind the Secret Science
Gemstone Journeys
Galactic Healing
Beyond Reality: Evidence of Parallel Universes

Videos:

Gemstone Journeys
Stones of Power

CD's

Origins of Huna: Ho'Oponopono
Journey to Spirit: Meeting Your Guides
Journey to Spirit: Abundance
Journey to Grief Recovery
Sacred Sounds
Lifestream: Journey Into Past & Future Lives
Healing with the Elements

Original music by Christine Cochrane

Titles available from:
Galactic Healing
www.galactichealing.org

As a wave,
Seething and foaming,
Is only water

So all creation,
Streaming out of the Self,
Is only the Self.

Consider a piece of cloth.
It is only threads!

So all creation,
When you look closely,
Is only the Self.

-Ashtavakra Gita 2:4-5

Acknowledgements

I would like to express my love and gratitude to the following people: Mickey, Gail and Mark Kaehr, Joe Crosson, Cheryl Doyle, Raymond and Cheryl Moody, Brian Weiss, and all of my clients whose stories are contained within these pages:

I Thank You!!

Contents

PART THREE – HEALING

Introduction

People often ask me how I got into my current profession and I will now address this in the following pages. This is the story of my journey and the stories of many of the people I have been fortunate enough to work with through the years in my private practice.

I have been working on this book in one form or another for nearly nine years. It describes a powerful process I developed called *Lifestream*, which is my own version of hypnotic regression.

After working with hundreds of people, over time, I

realized that the past-life regression alone was not all that was needed to gain a positive result that was both healing and empowering.

Lifestream is a three-part process. First, the person heals grief and present life relationships; next they journey into the past to discover and explore inner talents currently outside their conscious awareness; finally, they travel to the future to put all of the learning together while identifying the soul's purpose.

We will explore this phe-nomena through my own personal journey and the many case studies of my clients. In the last part of the book, the process will be revealed so you may experience it yourself.

My hope is that it will help you answer some of the deeper questions you have about yourself and find some comfort and healing in that process.

One
Opening

My spiritual journey began when I was a child. Many of the things I am now doing for a living were hobbies of mine at a young age. I was always fascinated by that which could not be seen, and that interest has only grown deeper as the years have gone on.

who decided to move out of state. After the move, he invited me to visit him one weekend to go hiking.

Timing was not good, so I decided to stay home, and on that weekend he was tragically killed in a hiking accident.

At the funeral home, I spoke aloud that I wanted to see him just once more to say good-bye.

As requested, my friend decided to fulfill my wish. One day after coming home from work, I happened to glance in the window of my house and saw him standing there in the window in a full form manifestation. It is rather hard to describe, but basically, he was translucent white and wore a white tank top and jeans. I wondered if that was what he was wearing at

the time of his death. It was a pleasant experience at first until the image began to change. It began to morph into a several layer image - each one showing a different emotion. The first was happy and smiling, the next was angry and the third sad as if all the emotions could be seen at once. It was very startling to look at, to say the least!

Over the next six months, he continued to make appearances. Once he made his presence known in a restaurant. I began to smell him and actually began to shed tears that were not my own. Another time, he appeared as a glowing outline in the back seat of my car while I was driving after dark.

Eventually I became completely overwhelmed by this presence. I ultimately concluded I was somehow to blame for inviting him to visit in the first place.

After deep prayer and meditation, I finally stopped having

encounters with the deceased spirit and began to get on with my life.

That is, until six years later when I began having the visitations again. This time, the presence was so strong, I asked some friends for advice. It was suggested I have a past-life regression because obviously this person had some kind of unfinished business with me.

Could I actually be holding up his soul's evolution in some way by not properly addressing him when he visited? I was unsure, but the possibility was enough to motivate me to look into it.

Two

My first trip to the past

I have always been fascinated by the possibility of past lives ever since I read the book *Bridey Murphy* when I was a young teen. In the book, a woman who suffered greatly from allergies went to a hypnotherapist to seek help and found that she had lived a past-life as a woman named Bridey Murphy in Ireland.

She had detailed descriptions of the lifetime that were so seemingly accurate, there would be little room to doubt the validity of her claims.

Since the book was released, there have been several debunkers who said the Bridey story was not real. It was brought to light that "Bridey" had a neighbor when she was a little girl who was an Irish immigrant. "Bridey's" life as she recalled it under hypnosis was strikingly similar to the life of her childhood neighbor.

Did the woman really live in Ireland in a past life or did she merely pick up information from her neighbor and store it in her unconscious mind so she could later transfer it on herself?

As far as I am concerned, that is a question that none of us can adequately answer until we check out of this place and head for the other side. It would be wrong of me to say here that is the way things are with any degree of certainty, because at this point in my evolution I can say no more about this subject than you can.

I will say that because of my past experiences and from speaking to others, I now believe past lives are indeed a very real possibility and one I have enjoyed looking into.

My first regression was actually nine years ago, shortly after my friend was killed in the hiking accident. I was at a 4th of July party at a friend's house and was introduced to a hypnotherapist.

One of my first questions of him was to ask if he knew how to do a past- life regression. He said he did and asked if I would like to see how it is done. The end result was that he was actually able to do the regression while I stood at the kitchen counter with people gathered around.

I quickly visited three lifetimes, the most prominent one being that of a gunslinger named John who lived in the 1860's.

Next, I saw cobblestone streets around the turn of the century, and in the third life, all I saw was a dark curtain drawn room.

All three lifetimes I saw were just like snapshots or seeing a fast slide show. "Look down at your feet," the hypnotherapist told me during the first experience. I was wearing cowboy boots and standing in the middle of some dusty town that looked a lot like an old western movie.

What was most puzzling was the fact that I was totally conscious of everything I was saying, yet I could not figure out where all of this "stuff" was coming from. That is the most common complaint from my own clients now

- they feel like they are making it all up. I tell them what I will tell you now - that reaction is "Perfect!"

When I came out of the trance, everybody who was witnessing this event began to call me "John," and I actually found myself turning my head a couple of times! I could not believe it!

What I also did not realize at that time was the significance of the three lives I had visited and the important role that discovery would later play in my own healing process.

Three
Back to the past

Six years later, my deceased friend began again to show up in my home. In life, he did not believe people should use electric blankets so during this round of visits, I would find that something or "someone" had mysteriously been turning off my blanket on one side only during the bitterly cold winter in Colorado.

After personally investigating the matter, I concluded this had to be his spirit. There was nobody else in the house.

This continued to happen and I again felt the presence and his smell strongly on numerous occasions, so I was inspired to believe there was something to it all when I happened to turn on a talk show one morning.

The show had a woman named Char Margolis on it. "Psychic Char," as she was called, was a gifted medium who began to describe people who would sense the presence of their departed loved ones by actually crying their tears and feeling their emotions.

This was long before John Edward was even discovered so it was something I had never heard being discussed in such an open forum as television.

After this, I knew that the

things I had seen in the past and the ones I was currently experiencing were not necessarily part of my possibly delusional mind, but that they may actually have some validity to them.

That is when I decided to employ a professional hypno-therapist to see what, if anything, was going on.

I remember feeling a bit apprehensive at first when I went to the appointment. There was a mixture of excitement and fear at finally being able to put an end to whatever was going on here.

The twenty-four hours prior to the appointment, I had been fasting. This was just coincidental, yet it was probably part of the reason this was, and continues to be to this day, the most powerful past-life experience I have ever had.

The therapist relaxed me and began counting down. When

she asked me to go back to the time when... I suddenly found myself feeling like I was in a tilt-o-whirl at a carnival. I was spinning around and around so fast I could not slow down. I felt like I was in space in some kind of a black hole spinning out of control.

Finally she asked me to come to the place where I first knew my friend. After what seemed to be a very long time, the spinning finally came to an end, and I stopped.

I felt myself being jerked into a big, heavy space. I could not see anything at first, and then I began to focus. My arms and hands felt heavy and as I was able to "look out my own eyes" I became aware that I was staring into a little cottage and I was standing out in the snow.

But why did my arms feel so heavy? I looked down and realized my arms were now huge. I had a big hood on made of skins of animals. I was a man! And a big man, at that!

"What year is it?" she asked.

"1868," I said.

"What is your name?"

As soon as the question was asked, I realized this was a life I already knew of. "John!" I was the same guy I had seen six years earlier, only now it was winter and a different scene from the same life.

I continued to stare into the windows of the little cabin as the snow fell around me.

"Nobody's there." I told the therapist.

"Where are they?" she asked.

"Gone."

"Go ahead and go back to a time when they were there."

I felt my tilt-o-whirl start up again but this time it moved slower and stopped in a few seconds.

"I am inside the cabin now."

"Is anybody there with you?"

"My family!" I said, as I looked at my wife and two kids.

I could smell food cooking. My WIFE! I instantly recognized who she was.

"He was my wife!" I told her.

"What happened to your

family?" she asked.

What I saw next was, again, like a slideshow. I saw

snapshots of the bloody bodies of my wife and kids on the floor. Apparently they had been killed while I was out hunting. I cried as I saw the devastating scene and felt the immense pain of the loss.

"Fast forward to the end of your life," the therapist directed.

"I died a lonely man. I never wanted anything to do with anybody from then on. My heart was broken. I was killed by a bear in the forest."

***

I was asked to review any other lifetimes we may have shared. Again I got into my time machine/tilt-o-whirl and went off to the next spot. The time was the turn of the century.

Again, it was a life I recognized from the party years before. In this lifetime, I was a young girl. It felt like I was living somewhere on the east coast of the United States.

Things here were very grim and I felt poor and destitute. It was basically the same scene at first as the one I saw six years earlier. I was walking around on cobble stone streets holding the hand of my little sister. We were going to visit our father who was working as a shoe cobbler.

After the brief review of the part I had seen before, the images expanded into new territory - to an earlier time. I saw myself in a kitchen with my mother, father and sister. Our mother was very ill.

"My mother gets sick and dies because we cannot afford proper medical treatment," I reported, almost in tears.

Lifestream

Now, my little sister was my sole responsibility.

I flashed next to a later time in a bedroom with curtains drawn. Somebody was gravely ill. It was my sister. She eventually died. I felt it was all my fault! There was nothing I could do to save her.

"He was MY SISTER!"

I recognized that my friend was my sister in this miserable lifetime. This was now the second life in a row where he had died and left me behind. Was there a pattern forming here?

***

The last stop on the journey in the time machine was to a lifetime in 1942. All I could see was a dark bedroom, this time in a totally new location.

There was a woman there

who was very ill. She was giving
birth to someone. I soon realized I
was seeing my own birth! The
woman was my mother, and
unfortunately, she died in childbirth.

"How did you feel about that?"
the therapist asked.

*"It was a guilt I carried with me
my entire life,"* I said.

I quickly came to a shocking realization: MY MOTHER! My
friend was my mother!

Clearly, there was a pattern
that had been established.

Three lives in the past, as
well as the life in the present had all
resulted in the soul of my friend
leaving my soul behind and feelings
of guilt and "What if?" consumed
my thoughts in each incident.

As I had suspected, there
was indeed a pattern here - a very
old, and unproductive one.

Over and over again as I work with clients I see that they too have patterns of behavior that are very old.

The discovery of such things is only the first part of the healing process. Later in part three, I will describe in detail how to heal wounds such as these with personal examples from clients and myself, and by using the *Lifestream* process.

Four
Value of
regression

So what good are regressions, anyhow, and why would somebody want to go through one? The reasons and positive results are boundless as you will see in the following pages.

Again, I must state that regardless of whether you believe this is possible or not, through the years and several hundred clients I have worked with, I have come to regard this as a stunningly powerful process of self-discovery, if nothing else.

As the hypnotist, I am merely a facilitator, or as I like to say, the "tour guide" to people's unconscious minds. As such, I do not offer suggestions to the client as to what they may or may not experience. I merely ask the questions and record the results.

All I can say about the process is that every person is as unique as the stars in the sky and each has a story to tell. The amazing things I hear are coming from the minds of the clients. They are originating from some place, but the question is where?

Some say the person was probably sitting in his or her play-pen as a baby and absorbing soap operas and other television pro-gramming subconsciously and, just as in the case of the woman in *Bridey Murphy*, they are now absorbing and attempting to become that which they were exposed to as a child.

I personally disagree with this philosophy. To me, the bottom line is whether the information gathered helped the person come to some deeper understanding of themselves so they may be empowered to live life more fully and get on to the business of what they were meant to do here.

As long as people feel better, that is my primary objective, and that is perfect. I challenge you as you read these next passages to keep your mind open to the fact that all things are possible.

The great prophet, Edgar Cayce spoke about the Akashic records. All of the experiences of each soul is recorded in the records and Cayce was able to tap into them to give life readings to people.

Cayce said himself that:

"Anyone may read these records if he can attune himself properly...really and truly, I do not believe there is a single individual that doesn't possess this same ability I have. I am certain that all human beings have much greater powers than they are ever conscious of - if they would only be willing to pay the price of detachment from self interests that it takes to develop these abilities."

Edgar Cayce's Story of Jesus, p.15

The joy of self-discovery is one of the things I want to teach people. I find that self-exploration leads us to a deep understanding of ourselves and that our personal journey is what helps us really get the lessons. We did not sign up for life to have all the answers handed to us on a silver platter, did we?

Lifestream

I recently saw Carolyn Myss give a lecture on her groundbreaking work *Sacred Contracts*. One of the points made in that work is that we all think we want to know the answers to all of life's deepest questions, such as:

Who will I marry?

What will I do for a living that will make me rich and happy 100% of the time?

The truth is that if we knew these things instantly and they were handed to us, we would soon be bored stiff!

We live for the path and the journey! It makes us always strive to improve ourselves.

One of the things that was most difficult about my friend's death I mentioned at the beginning of the book is that when it happened, at age 27, I had never seen a dead body before, and had never attended a funeral!

Many people experience death quite frequently and often early in life. I often wonder why we all choose the paths we are on and why some people go through certain things while others do not. I used to feel "lucky" to have avoided the wrath of the grim reaper for most of my life, yet at the time I wished I had experienced it earlier because the pain of inexperience was hard to bear.

I suppose this is a cosmic question we all ask from time to time: why are some born to "suffer" while others seem to be on "easy street?" I believe regressions offer ways to explore this thoroughly and help us accept things we go through in life, and the "injustices" we see on a daily basis.

There was a writing I saw many years ago about a so-called

hierarchy of needs. It was a chart that looked like a pyramid. The base of the pyramid showed basic survival needs - food, shelter, and clothing. As the chart progressed toward the top of the pyramid, the needs become more of a worldly and spiritual nature.

In my opinion, the purpose of such a chart is to show that soul must have many different kinds of experiences over many lifetimes. Clients often see themselves as wealthy rulers in one lifetime and paupers in the next.

At a soul level, we came here to learn about all types of things and therefore we must experience all types of realities.

That is what makes people so interesting!

This idea also helps one come to terms with the world and the things we tend to label as "good" or "bad." The truth is that life is what it is - it is not for us to judge. Everything we go through is part of the learning process that each soul chose before they got here.

There are many other reasons why I feel regressions are a valid tool for self-analysis, which we will continue to explore.

Five
Famous People

One other reason regression is valid to me is that rarely do I ever meet the souls of famous people.

Certainly we cannot all be Napoleon or Cleopatra, right? That would seem a bit much. There are times, though, when these types of experiences do come up in a session.

One of the most memorable was a young man who came for a regression and was transported back to the days when he recalled being James of the Bible. He described the scenery of Biblical times rather convincingly and seemed to have a fair amount of detail about events.

In this case, I was skeptical for several reasons. First, there is the obvious fact that all of us have been so ingrained with Biblical stories through the years that they would be easy to replicate.

Next, James has been in the news lately. In Jerusalem, archae-ologists have recently discovered a bone box containing the remains of what may be Jesus' brother James.

The translation of the inscription on the box reads: *"James, son of Joseph, brother of Jesus."*

Lifestream

Scholars seem to think this is the real thing. Perhaps my client saw this in the news.

I decided to question him afterwards about his experience as James.

It was during the post session that I was able to uncover that a local psychic told him he was James.

I am sure this revelation played well with his ego, so he decided to adapt it as his own. This is what I mean by the person being robbed of having an experience when they are given the answers to the questions they ask, because it is so easy to have the ego set in, especially if the life is appealing to us.

In my career, I have encountered Nefertiti, Queen of Egypt, on more than one occasion.

What is the likelihood in a world of over a billion people to run into Nefertiti more than once in the same town?

I also regressed others who were simply in the company of famous people. One man journeyed with Socrates through Greece and was one of his close advisors. I found his attention to detail seemed stunningly accurate and had me convinced for awhile that he may have been who he claimed. My only doubt came with my discovery of the fact that he was a university professor of philosophy.

I also heard about a paranoid schitzophernic who claims to be the reincarnation of Julius Caesar. Is it possible? Maybe!

So what would cause people to identify so closely with these historic figures?

Are they tapping into the collective consciousness? As the late Carl Jung pointed out, mass thought creates energetic patterns in the universe that can be accessed by us all. Perhaps these clients were tapping into the collective consciousness of the historic figure they wish to be, or the archetypal energy they are working with in this lifetime.

Thought creates. We become that which we think about.

Certainly there is nothing wrong with thinking you are the reincarnated version of a great holy man from the Bible! I would think this could inspire one to be on his or her very best behavior in order to continue to meet and exceed high Biblical standards and that the person would be compelled to treat people decently and with respect so as to not disgrace the name of the one he or she has chosen to identify with.

The world could be at peace if we could all reach in to find the best parts of ourselves! On the other hand, what would happen if you were told you were actually Attila the Hun?

The other thought I have on this topic is that maybe the one they think they are is actually a spirit guide. In my first book *Origins of Huna: Secret Behind the Secret Science* I tell my experience of being visited by a man who died thirty years ago and came back from beyond the grave to lead me to a secret.

So if I can believe this is possible, certainly it is also possible to believe I may have actually regressed the reincarnation of James!

All of our speculation will eventually be answered when we reach the other side. Until then, it is interesting to think about all of the infinite possibilities.

Six
Relationships

One of the most common reasons people seek past-life regression is because they are having some difficulty understanding the complexities of a relationship.

At one point, I wanted to call this book *Karmic Obsession* because I believe we often find ourselves mixed up in messy relationships with people we know we should not be with, but because of a deep tie to the past, we find we cannot break free.

One example of this exact scenario is a woman who came in to see me who had recently started dating someone. When she called to set the appointment she told me she was coming to help figure out what was going on with this man. I knew it would be an interesting session.

When she came into the office, she soon admitted that she was originally not attracted at all to this person but found herself in a relationship with him and was battling her inner confusion over the whole situation. He treated her well and with respect, yet there was a nagging feeling she could not quite figure out.

In the regression it was discovered that they were very

old acquaintances. In one life in the 1700's, her boyfriend was a king and she had an affair with him. She lived her life loving him secretly while he disrespected her and in the end, on her deathbed, she realized he never cared for her at all.

In the second lifetime we explored, she lived in Egypt and her current boyfriend was her servant. She loved him but decided to marry the man who was chosen for her in order to spare unnecessary hardship for her people. It was another situation where the two of them could not be together.

So what is the answer then? Are the two lovers just meant to cross paths but never get together in any lifetime? Or is this the life where they will finally get together and "live happily ever after?"

That is for the client to decide and in this case, I do not know how it ended.

In most sessions the best

choice is revealed by using the *Lifestream* process I will show you later in the book.

Even after the best choice is clearly shown, it is ultimately the client who must choose whether or not to follow his or her own advice.

***

People are often surprised by what comes up during a session. One woman came in out of curiosity and was amazed at what she found out about one of her most challenging relationships in this lifetime.

"What are you wearing?" I asked her.

"Victorian petticoats with a lace hat, and my hair is in sausage curls. I am riding in a carriage

and seem to be well to do. There is somebody waiting for me to get in. We ride around and all the houses are tall and very close together."

"What year is it?"

"1824."

"What else is happening?"

"I am going to a country side store, like a cottage. My grandmother is there and she's come to see me. She is plump and has rosy cheeks and I am hugging her."

"What else?"

"We are baking bread."

"How old are you?"

"Eighteen."

"Is there anyone else there with you?"

"Grandfather just came in. He is smoking a pipe. They love me and they are pouring tea for me. It is really nice. I wonder why I am there though."

"Where are you?"

"England."

"Fast forward to the next most significant event of this lifetime. What is happening now?"

"There are horses being brought around, but I sense danger. They bring a spirited horse for me to ride."

"How do you feel about that?"
I asked.

"I'm afraid."

Lifestream

"What happens next?"

" There is a man holding horses for both of us. There seems to be a companion or brother figure there. I am getting angry because he is making me do this. I won't show him I'm angry."

"As you look around at all the people you've seen in this lifetime, is there anyone who seems familiar to you?"

"Yes, the brother is my brother in this lifetime."

"Okay, now what is happening?"

"I am so angry at him but I am also determined.... I've fallen off! Now I am in a four poster bed ith lots of pillows and comforters. The light from the window is too bright."

"Fast forward to the next most significant event of this lifetime."

"I am not the same after I recover. It changed me - made me stronger and maybe meaner. My brother showed no remorse, but I never let him push me around again! I eventually became estranged from him and we really did not speak again."

It was later determined that in the current lifetime the woman and her brother had a falling out and were not on speaking terms.

Again, an old pattern was being replayed in a new time.

***

Another woman was seeking answers about relationships in the past she said were "very unhealthy." She told me she had been seeing someone for the past six months and could not get out of it and wanted to know who he was in the past. She discovered the two had met in the late 1800's.

"We lived in a big white house and had three children. He does not pay any attention to me anymore like he did when we were first married. He did not like being married. He wanted his freedom, so he left."

"What is the lesson you were to have learned and how does it apply to the current situation?" I asked.

"I have to let him go, I'll be stuck. It is a pattern," she said.

The woman seemed to realize what she thought would be best for her in the given situation. The question is whether or not she will take her own advice.

     We all have choices. I will tell you what she chose later in the book.

Seven
Health

One of the main reasons I got into the alternative health field was because I survived a very long illness and felt I had garnered tools along the way I could use to help others.

For me, holding on to the energetic patterns of the past was one of the things that was killing me slowly in this lifetime. Past patterns actually hold space in the physical body, which I discovered firsthand.

With each lifetime I explored and healed, there seemed to be some energetic release, which you may also experience yourself in the last part of the book.

I actually felt myself get a kind of energetic circulation in places where I did not have it before.

Blood rushed through my face and limbs and I was relieved of a burden that was previously outside my conscious awareness.

That is why it is not surprising that so many people come to my office because of serious health issues. They use regression as a last resort when all else fails.

One of the most interesting people I ever met was a woman who was plagued by poor health in this lifetime and had come to see me with a list of things to discover about herself.

She had been in a car wreck in her teens in this lifetime, and was accidentally declared dead.

She woke up in a body bag as she was being carried down to a morgue!! She screamed hysterically and was fortunately discovered and released.

I've heard stories about people accidentally being buried alive in the old days and that upon exhuming the graves, scratch marks are often found on the inside of the coffin lids.

Until I met this woman though, I had not heard of any such thing taking place in modern times. The situation definitely piqued my interest: what did *she* come here to learn?

When I saw her, she had a broken sternum that would not heal, acute liver problems, weak bones and problems with an ear.

I discovered she lived in the early 1900's when she fell down a flight of stairs and broke her neck. The realization of this actually helped her sternum to heal.

I have a similar story to tell about myself. When I was born in my current incarnation, I suffered from acute kidney failure and was not expected to live.

In further explorations of my prior lifetime in 1942, I discovered that I became a melancholy soul after losing my mother in childbirth, so I apparently drank myself to death.

Potentially, those health problems could have carried over into my current lifetime.

This phenomena is called *miasm*. The miasm is where we actually carry an energetic blockage straight in from a previous lifetime to our current incarnation and it will usually create an illness, often in childhood.

Miasms can be corrected with past-life regression. Often the simple discovery of a past relationship to the current illness will be enough to release the energetic blockage that originally created it.

I discovered other miasms when working with clients. One story that particularly stood out was a man who came in with hypertension, also known as high blood pressure.

I asked him to go back to the time when the high blood pressure became a concern for him and he wound up back in a relatively recent lifetime in 1942.

"What do you see?" I asked.

"I am in a uniform and I am sitting in the cockpit of a B-17. I am the copilot."

"What is happening?'

"It is foggy out and we can't see from the fog. We are hit. I get the impression that both engines on the right side are out. The plane is going down slowly. I instruct the crew to bail. We are flying over Germany."

"How do you feel?"

"My heart is racing out of control."

"Now what happens?"

"The plane broke up before I could get out. We crashed. I am hurt bad and am bleeding. The captain is dead."

This is also another example of miasm. The high blood pressure had been an unexplainable problem for this client at an unusually early age, yet it was due to the incident in the previous lifetime.

Lifestream

Like me, this person was also "reborn" from 1942 into the current lifetime in the 1960's.

Taking a look into the past can very often provide answers to previously puzzling medical conditions.

As for the woman with the broken sternum, she eventually healed many of her physical alments simply by reliving those incidents and healing from her past.

Eight
Addictions

Speaking of my prior life as an alcoholic, I have gained even further insight into myself through this exploration. In my current life, with the exception of a few years in college, I have no desire to drink, yet I have many friends who are in recovery from addictions to drugs and alcohol.

In my own session where I explored this, I told the therapist that I was here to befriend and offer support to those who suffered from substance abuse as part of what my soul came here to experience. It has been an interesting part of my journey.

As such, I often work with people who are in recovery, or who have been involved with people who abuse alcohol.

One woman who was a practicing alcoholic visited several lifetimes in which she was also a heavy drinker.

In one, she was a man who lived in the middle ages and died of consumption.

"That's just what we did in those days is drink. I suppose that is what led to my death," she said.

In another lifetime, she was living in England in a family that was extremely wealthy. Again she was the father and abused alcohol regularly.

"I was pretty mean. I was not very nice to my kids at all and I drank all the time. I did not mean to be that way, it was just how it was, I guess." she said.

Another man came in who wanted to know why he was continually getting involved with alcohol abusers in this lifetime.

Sure enough, in the past, his current girlfriend was his wife in a life in the early 1900's and he was the one who abused alcohol in that lifetime. Apparently, they were just reliving some old pattern of behavior.

Can delving into the past really heal the addiction and abuse? We will take a closer look at that possibility later in the book.

Nine
Grief recovery

Another of the reasons I chose to explore regression myself was as a tool in grief recovery. Now as a result of that, I would say that over 50% of my clients are dealing with some sort of grief when they come in for a session.

One woman in particular was suffering from severe grief

after the loss of her mother to cancer and the tragic murder of her brother, both a short time apart.

In the regression, she realized that in an earlier life in the 1940's, she knew her mother and brother because they were her parents in that lifetime.

"I am a little boy. I am wearing a red and white striped shirt and I am playing in a field with green grass and rolling hills all around. There are a lot of other kids playing too. My parents are there."

"What year is it?" I ask.

"It is somewhere in the '40's or '50's."

"What happens next?"

"There is a man there - it is my

dad. He is waiting for me to get done playing so we can go home. All my other brothers and sisters are at home. He is waiting for me to cross the street but I do not see the car. My dad watched me get hit. I get killed."

So in the lifetime in the 1940's, the woman left her mother and brother's spirits behind, so now in the current lifetime they are doing this to her.

The duality of that which we came to experience may not make the grief any less severe, but at least for myself and other clients, it seems to help one come to a greater amount of acceptance about why we have to deal with certain things in our lifetimes.

We do not have to like what has happened, but we can at least see the cosmic pattern of it.

Almost every person who comes in for a session is dealing

with some sort of loss. The healing potential using the *Lifestream* process is unlimited, and we will explore this at a much deeper level in part three of the book.

Ten

Spirituality

One of my favorite stories to tell is about a great friend of mine who is a professed Atheist. I have always found this peculiar and a bit depressing that somebody could believe that after this, there is nothing. To me, it would be an extremely frightening way to live if we did not have something to look forward to, yet, I respect his right to do and think as he wishes.

This gentleman is one of my favorite people because he is the consummate devil's advocate. There is nothing I like better than to prove him wrong, as he enjoys doing to me. It is a friendly and entertaining rivalry.

Since he always wants to debunk anything spiritual, he asked me to do a past-life regression on him, I assumed to try and discredit me.

I thought it was rather odd, with his beliefs, and reluctantly agreed to it since it was a total oxymoron to believe that one could have a past life and be a professed Atheist all at the same time. The two concepts could not both exist. If we lived before, that would assume that we are more than just dust and dirt after death. Reincarnation presupposes the concept of survival of bodily death.

What is also most interesting about my friend is that he has what I would call a Civil War "fetish."

I used to have a huge annual Halloween costume party at my house with hundreds of people. My friend and one of his buddies would always come every year decked out in full uniform of the confederacy.

His wife, who is also one of my closest friends, confided in me about a dream her husband had in which he was looking out his own eyes and was fighting on a battle-field in a uniform similar to those worn in the Civil War. He apparently woke up in a sweat, crying out, and was deeply disturbed for quite awhile afterwards.

Since I am a very curious person, I was anxious to try this regression, even though he was a nay-sayer, I felt I was up to the challenge of attempting to draw a past life memory from his unconscious mind.

He recalled a scene in which he was looking out a window, and saw Confederate soldiers down below.

"Where are you?" I asked.

"I am looking out of a window of a building. Like an upstairs of a house."

"Is it your house?"

"Yes."

"What are you looking at?"

"I am just looking down in to the street and watching the Confederate soldiers go by."

As he looked at them, he realized something shocking.

"What do you do for a living?"

Lifestream

"I am a soldier too, but not for the Confederacy."

My friend told me that, much to his surprise, he was actually a Union soldier!

He said that his fascination with the Confederacy stemmed from the fact that as he watched them, he felt that they really believed in their cause in a way that he did not.

He did not want to go to war and felt forced into it. He longed for a passionate belief in what he was doing which was currently missing from his work.

"They really believed in what they were doing. I wish I could feel like that." he said, sadly.

The bottom line of this endeavor was that as my "Atheist" friend recounted a prior lifetime, his paradigms of how he viewed the world were completely shattered.

He was so stunned that he was literally speechless and has never mentioned the episode again, to this day.

The reality of a past-life regression, regardless of whether or not it can be scientifically proven, is that it creates dramatic shifts in a person's concept of spirituality and the world we live in. One must reevaluate his place in the world after undergoing such a process, because it forces us to think of the vastness of our souls.

Eleven

Future lives and memories

Earlier, I mentioned a process that allows a person to see the best choice for their soul, and then act on it. These answers lie within the realm of future lives.

As I was developing the *Lifestream* process, it became clear that looking at the future was as important, if not more so, than looking into the past.

Most people are unaware that we actually have "memories" of future events and those things can be tapped into as easily as the past-life recollections.

I believe the purpose for looking at one's past is to use it as a tool to analyze patterns of behavior so one may be more empowered in the future.

I personally encourage myself and others to learn from the past, but not to dwell on it.

I have had people call me with concerns that having a past-life regression may cause them to become stuck.

Using the process of *Lifestream*, clients are not stuck. They are engaged in the recollection of certain skills and gifts used in the distant past that may be called upon and remembered and put to use in the future. Future life journeys allow people to instantly see how past life skills can be brought into the future.

The answers to all of the great mysteries of the soul are already within each of us. This process merely allows us to re-member who we are and recall our innate magnificence.

The Akashic record is not only a record of the past, but because it is a soul record, it is a record for all time.

So in essence, *Lifestream* is a process which empowers the client to make his or her own discoveries by reading their own soul records and enabling them to make more conscious decisions about the future by using their own unique wisdom from the past.

This is a great tool for goal setting because you actually have an opportunity to glimpse possible futures to see what may happen.

We must remember that the future is always open for change. It is constantly changing and every choice we make leads us to the next. There are infinite possibilities open to each of us at any given moment.

I believe we are potentially destined to do certain things, yet one decision or one fork in the road can lead us on an entirely different *Lifestream*.

When a client comes in, I do a soul reading on them, and I can see their highest potential. This helps me to facilitate the journey they are about to take and helps them to see the path that would lead to their highest good.

The choice still lies within each individual as to whether or not he or she is going to follow their own advice after making these discoveries. Just because someone can follow a certain path and be all they can be does not mean they will do it. It is all about choice.

Lifestream

Speaking of possibilities, I must interject here my opinion about how psychic information should be interpreted.

If we believe in the philosophy that all time is now, then everything is happening at once, and future memories are absolutely possible.

When we go to get our cards read, or ask someone for intuitive advice, what they are doing for us is tapping into our possible futures and glimpsing one or more of them.

We are all in charge here to a certain extent, and so when we receive this information we need to understand that we have within us the power to change what is going to happen. It is as if you continue down the path you are on, doing these same things, then this is *likely* to happen - not set in stone, but *possible*. However, you could chose differently and then that choice you make will open up a completely different realm of new opportunity.

Most people occasionally need someone to guide them to the "right" direction. I put the word "right" in quotes here because I do not believe in a total concept of what is the "right" decision verses the "wrong" one.

Even our darkest hours are actually the most powerful teachers - assuming we actually learn the lesson and stop repeating the perceived mistake.

During a future journey, there is always a path to choose from that is "lighter" or seemingly "easier" than another. Each can be seen clearly by the person so they may make the choice that is best - or not!

One of the most amazing future *Lifestream* journeys I ever had involved a client who is a practicing alcoholic.

Lifestream

She came to me to quit drinking. She said that she had been trying for years to stop, and had tried everything from rehab to going cold turkey, to substituting food, but nothing worked.

I knew things would have to become very painful for her to be motivated enough to change the habit. It is sad but true that none of us change unless things are painful. Sure, we may make small adjustments once in a while, but real, solid, life affirming changes are often a result of the heat getting too hot from the fire.

In this case, I used a process where I have the person travel over their time line, as if it was a beam of laser light. You will have the opportunity to try it yourself at the end of the book.

The person imagines looking out into the future and seeing it. In this case, I had her imagine she was staring at a huge fork in the road. One side representing the path she would take as a sober person, the other showing what would happen if the drinking continued.

To take the positive first, I had her look out in the future and travel to an unspecified point in the future to show her successfully off alcohol and happily completing her life's purpose.

She immediately flashed forward to a spot where she was addressing a large group. She was a teacher and was inspiring others to get off controlled substances. She was the living example of what she taught and was a pillar of her community.

Next, we needed to examine a possibly more painful glimpse of the future should the alcohol abuse continue.

She jumped forward to a rainy day. She could see a car that was smashed up and an ambulance. She realized that she had run into the car with her vehicle and that she was being arrested for drunk driving.

I decided to have her stay in the moment to see what happened to the people in the car.

"It was a family. A mother, father and a teenage boy. They are dead. I killed them. They are putting them in body bags."

"And what happens to you?"

"I see myself in prison, in an orange jumpsuit. I get sentenced to life in prison but end up getting out a bit early for good behavior, but I spent most of my life there."

After all of that, I am sure you would like to hear that the woman stopped her drinking and turned over a new leaf. For awhile it worked, yet I am sorry to say the change did not last.

Now back to the woman I mentioned in Chapter 6 who had a choice to make about whether or not to keep her current relationship. She traveled down the timeline into the future to a fork in the road.

One side of the fork showed what would happen if she continued her relationship with this man; the other side showed another possible reality without him. She could see for herself which to take.

"Which one of the paths is lighter?" I asked.

"The one to the right - the one without him. The path to the left looks dark and spiraling. The other one is straight and light." she said.

"Go down the path to the left now, and tell me what you see."

"I see us in a room. He is really rude and very disrespectful to me."

"What year is it?"

"2013."

"How do you feel?"

"I am unhappy. There is no passion, just like now," she admitted.

"Now go down the other side and tell me what is happening there."

"I live in a big house. It is a good life."

"What year is it?" I asked.

"2008," she said.

"How do you feel about this life

compared to the other one?"

"There is no doubt, this one is much better."

Clearly, there is a better choice to make in both of these situations. By better, I really mean lighter or less karmic. Ultimately, there is no wrong or right. We are the ones judging everything. There is a path for all of us that is less painful, though and that is what each one of us must decide - which path to go down.

What the people choose ultimately, though, is strictly up to them.

It is all about choice and each of us has that power.

Twelve
Healing the past

In the beginning of the book, I told the story of my friend who was killed in the hiking accident, and I mentioned that there was tremendous healing that took place in the process of discovering the ties we shared in the past.

This was only one aspect of the total healing that occurred. The other thing that led to tremendous personal growth was the process I will now share with you.

"I want you to imagine him standing in front of you now," the therapist said.

At first, I thought this was silly but went along with it. I was able to picture my friend walking out in front of me. It seemed like I was just imagining it.

"Is he there?" she asked after I did not answer.

"Yes," I said.

"Good. Now I want you talk to him and tell him how you feel about him leaving. How do you feel?"

"I suppose I feel guilty," I said. *"I have always felt that way."*

Lifestream

"Bring out your wife, your sister and your mother too and talk to each of them and let them know how you feel. If you want, tell them you are sorry. See what they say."

I thought I was making it all up, but sure enough, the wife, little sister and mother all came out and one by one I was able to make peace with them and realized they were not upset with me at all!

"Now ask your friend if he has anything that belongs to you, and if so, have him put it out on his hands so you can see it," she said.

I was really going to have to stretch to imagine this one, I thought. I doubted I would be able to see a thing. What happened next amazed me.

"What's going on? the therapist asked.

"He has something! He has my heart!" I said.

Sure enough when my friend put out his hands there was a heart in them. It looked just like the beating organ - it was not a symbolic experience at all which was quite a shock!

"Now I want you to take it back and put it inside," she said.

I did it and I put it up to my chest and immediately felt an energetic shift in my body that was uncanny. This seemed like it was "pretend," yet it felt so real. I felt better instantly.

***

This process made such a positive impact on my life I knew I had to share it with others. Now I never do a session without doing some version of this with clients, and it has evolved into one of the major components of *Lifestream*.

Usually before actually taking the client into the past-life recall mode, I take them first to a safe space in nature. It is here I have found that many of them seem to connect with their deceased relatives, or estranged family members and the process can take place.

Potentially, the people who meet the client in this special space are souls who they have known before. The soul connection of the people who appear here is so strong, it is only natural that they have come here to share many lifetimes together.

You will recall earlier in Chapter 9, I mentioned the story

about the woman who was suffering from a terrible case of grief after the death of her mother who died of cancer, and her brother who was murdered.

While visiting the safe space, we were both overcome by the spiritual presence of them both as they came into the room.

I told her they were here with us and she said she could "see" them in her mind's eye.

I had her ask each of them to give back what they had that belonged to her. She told me that her brother had a piece of her heart and her mother had her confidence to stand and face the world. She felt abandoned and alone since their death and needed to reclaim her security in the world without them.

I told her to put them back inside and feel how much better she felt. I could see her face relax and she did appear to feel better. Then we did another process which can

also ease the devastation of acute grief.

Lifestream

"I want you to imagine you can reach out and hold them both. Put your arms around them and bring them so close. Imagine they are right here. They have never left. I want you to totally reconnect with their energy."

She did that, and again, the energetic shift was immediate and profound. I believe that the devastation of grief comes primarily from the sickening feeling we have that we will never be in the presence of our loved one again and that is what can be so overwhelming to most people.

***

When we facilitate our soul's recollection of the fact that we are all one and that there really

is no separation, we can immediately feel better.

I remind people that in my opinion, the deceased may not be so far away after all, perhaps they are merely in another dimension, or they may now be vibrating at a higher frequency, which is currently unperceivable to most people, but not all.

I believe that is why some people can sense the dead because they can see, feel or hear that which is out of the range of most people, yet it is something we all have the ability to do.

With practice and focused intent, anyone can have this type of experience and maybe you already have, you may just have not been aware of it at the time. Try it!

***

The other use for this process is to heal current relationships with the living. Often some of our toughest lessons we come here to learn are with the people we have the most difficulty getting along with.

Earlier, I spoke of the woman whose brother in a past life coerced her into riding a wild horse and as a result, she was severely injured. In this lifetime, the two had been estranged for several years after the death of their father.

We did a process similar to the one I mention in my first book, *Origins of Huna*, where I had her imagine her brother in front of her and that the two of them could forgive each other and be thankful for the fact that they came here to learn lessons together. Then, she was asked to cut an imaginary cord between them that symbolized all of the ill will of the past. She was asked to let it all go!

This process is called healing the part of you that is

someone else. As mentioned earlier, we are all a part of the same energy field so when we are able to forgive and forget, we actually create a real energetic shift in the universe.

This process, like so much of what I do, seems like pretend. It seems like a nice fantasy, but nothing that is rooted at all in reality. There could be nothing further from the truth!

The very next day after her session, her brother "happened" to call her after they had not spoken at all for the past five years!! Coincidence? Hardly!

***

Lifestream

One of the most amazing healings I ever experienced using this process was a man who came in to see me concerning his health problems.

He was suffering from acute kidney and congestive heart failure, and was on the waiting list to receive a kidney transplant.

As we began the *Lifestream* journey, he went to the beautiful place in nature and was surprised to see his deceased mother and father there.

"It's like I am in a canopy of trees and I could see the sunlight through the trees. The leaves are golden and green and make a strange color light like a glow. There are leaves on the ground and there are a lot of herbs growing there on the trees. I feel so relaxed, it almost feels like I am floating. Here I am in perfect

health. They came up holding hands which was strange because they died 20 years apart. They looked like they were 35 or 40.

My mother didn't look old anymore. She looked as young as she was when my father was still alive and all the worry lines were gone from her face. It was like they were both at peace with the world.

That made me feel good since he died alone at work and when she died she was alone in the hospital dying of cancer and it was nice they were there together because she really loved him. He was the love of her life. It was good to see them together again.

All of that gives me hope that we do find happiness in another world and that our soul does not just die here, we keep it wherever we go."

Lifestream

During the session the man realized he was still angry at his parents for not taking good care of themselves and dying too young.

"They apologized to me but they told me that they were finished with what they came here to do so it was just their time to go. Once they were done with their purpose here they were done. Apparently, you don't linger. There was really nothing to be angry about at all. It is some sort of law of the universe, or something. When they talked to me it was not really in words, it was like in thoughts."

Since the man's father died when he was a young boy, the eight-year old version of him came out to address his father.

"When the younger me came out

*he came up and held my father's
hand. Up until that time, I was
devoted to my father completely
and hung on every word he said.
The younger me was really happy
to see him."*

Soon afterwards, the
client's own children appeared, and
they told him they were upset
because he was not properly taking
care of himself, just like his parents
did when he was young. There is
an old saying about "the sins of the
father" and this was applicable in
this situation. No wonder the man
was in poor health, he learned how
to take care of himself from his
parents who did not take good care
of themselves.

*"It was surprising that my kids
showed up there. They hugged
me a lot and told me they did not
want me to go and to take better*

*care of myself. I told them I was
taking better care of myself."*

    Then all the family members
held hands and hugged each other.
    After the session, the man
described his experience further.

*"I could actually smell my father
and mother. It was really powerful."*

    This is a powerful example
of how generations of a family can
experience a great healing.
    Regardless of whether or
not family members are alive or
deceased, they can meet in this
space and resolve many situations
in a very short period of time.
    When we heal ourselves we
really do heal our entire family for
future and past generations.

Thirteen

Energy & Soul Memory

One of the reasons *Lifestream* is so powerful is because it involves the use of energy healing in addition to the verbal exercises the client goes through.

Many people who come to the office tell me they tried hypnosis before and it did not work because

they were unable concentrate.
That is one of the reasons I com-
bine the technique with energy
healing. I first learned about using
energy work in combination with
the guided imagery when I was out
working at large expos. Hundreds
of people would walk by my booth
and it was often very noisy, yet I
found when I would put the palms
of my hands into people's auras and
began to tune into their energy
fields, it was much easier for them
to concentrate.

"I heard the noise from all
the people when we first started,
but then it seemed to become dull,
almost like background music or
something. I was really relaxed and
could only hear your voice. I
almost forgot I was sitting in the
middle of a big convention center,"
one woman told me.

The other aspect of
Lifestream that makes it unique is

a journey that clients go on to a special place where they are able to identify their soul's purpose.

Clients are asked to float to the beginning of time where they are met by angels, their spirit guides or God himself.

In this space, clients are able to ask questions of these beings about their soul purpose - a decision they made as a soul about what lessons or things they would like to learn about over the course of many lifetimes.

This is one of the main places where, in my opinion, the people are actually accessing information from their own Akashic, or soul, record. Amazingly, people can tell me exactly why they are here, and how they will go about actualizing this purpose in their current lifetime.

I again ask the question, then, about why people would

need to consult psychics for intuitive advice when they actually have all the answers within themselves. It is merely a matter of teaching them how to access the information.

The mind and the memory of the soul are like a massive computer. You can have all the answers contained in sophisticated programming and software, yet it is worthless if you are unable to figure out how to turn the computer on and off. This exercise is the roadmap by which people can know the inner most desires of their souls and remember the divine beings they really are and how they will most eloquently express their special inborn gifts and talents to the world.

When I ask people to tell me their soul's purpose, the most common answer I hear is that the person came here to learn about LOVE, and has been learning about that in many lifetimes.

Lifestream

Often it is a lack of love or a relationship challenge that brought them to me in the first place.

Yet it is pointed out by their spirit guides that learning about how not to love is indeed part of getting to know what love really is. We are the ones who judge ourselves and others about the things we do.

We have the power to decide if we want to learn how to love in a positive or negative way. Either way, the lesson is learned.

Fourteen
Lifestream

Now is the time you have been waiting for. I have spent the last several chapters describing many of the possible outcomes of the *Lifestream* process and now it is time for you to try it for yourself.

The following pages contain the scripts for your journey to past, present and future. You can do this process as often as you would like.

EXERCISE

Here is the exercise you can try yourself at home.

If possible, record this and play it back to yourself.

There are three parts so after going through the initial relaxation part you can do any one or all of these exercises whenever you want.

They do not have to de done all at once.

RELAXATION

Go ahead and sit down in a comfortable chair with your feet on the floor and your hands on your lap.

Take a deep, relaxing breath as you close your eyes and begin to imagine a beam of pure white light going down in through the top of your head.

Lifestream

Allow the white light to move into your face - your eyes, nose, jaw, and down into your neck. Allow the white light to heal you and relax you as it moves into your shoulders - your elbows, wrists, hands and down into your fingertips.

Allow the white light to continue to move down into your shoulders and back, your chest and stomach, into your legs - your thighs, knees, calves and down into your feet.

Imagine the white light is pouring through you like a waterfall, carrying any tension and concerns you have and moving it down toward the ground and out the soles of your feet, into the earth.

Imagine the light becoming more and more powerful. So powerful it begins to pour out of your heart, creating a golden ball of light that surrounds you by about 3 feet in all directions.

Imagine feeling the healing warmth of this golden light as it surrounds you and heals you and know that inside the golden ball only that which is of your highest good can get through.

Now imagine a doorway in front of you. See it, feel it, or just allow yourself to have an inner knowing that it is there.

HEALING THE HEART

Imagine you can walk through that door now and as you do, you find yourself inside a beautiful room. Look around and see what's there.

Notice the good vibrations of this place as you begin to explore your surroundings.

Lifestream

As you look around, you notice there is another doorway at the other side of the room. Go over there and open that door. As you do, you notice you are about to step outside to a beautiful place in nature. Go ahead now and walk outside.

Notice if it is a sunny day or a cloudy day.. Notice if there are any birds, or animals around. Are there any mountains or bodies of water?

As you begin to notice your surroundings, you see a tree off in the distance. Go ahead now and walk toward the tree. Imagine you can put your back against the tree as you relax even more and enjoy this special place - your favorite place - in nature.

Now I want you to imagine that somebody who is very special to you is walking up to you now. The person may be *alive now, or it may be someone who has already passed into spirit.*

Say hello to this person and thank them for visiting you today. Imagine that this is the higher part of the person - their soul - talking to the higher part of you.

Imagine you could take time now to thank each other for all of the lessons you came here to learn.

If necessary, imagine you could apologize to each other for any misunderstandings and take time to discuss anything else that may need to be said.

Now I want you to ask them if they have anything that belongs to you, and if so, have them put it out on their hands so you can see it.

Notice what is there. How do you feel about that? Now imagine you can reach out

and bring that back inside
yourself.   That's right.   Go ahead
and put it back inside.

Now imagine a blinding
white light coming down again
into the top of your head.   Allow
the light to go down into every
cell of your body and into your
heart.

Imagine the light is like a
welder's torch, melting the cracks
and breaks in the heart and
molding them back into a state of
total perfection now.

Notice how much better
you feel - how complete you feel
now.

Now notice if you have
anything that belongs to them
and if so, put it out on your
hands.   Allow them to take it
from you and bring it back inside.

Notice how much lighter
you feel! The weight of the world
is gone!

Allow the healing white

Shelley Kaehr, Ph.D.

*light to move in through the
other person and give them the
same type of healing you had.
Now also imagine the light
moving once again through you
and filling in the space created by
this thing you gave back.*

*Notice how much better
you feel!*

*If the person is someone
who is no longer in your life
because they have either passed
away or are far away from you,
take a moment now to imagine
that you could put your arms
around them and just hold them.
Allow every cell of your body to
totally reconnect with their
energy now.*

*They are right here! They
were never gone! The separation
was just an illusion. Allow
yourself to realize that they are
closer to you than you thought.*

*Feel the relief of no
longer being separated from the*

love of this special person.

When you feel totally reconnected to this person, imagine you could stand back again and as you do, you will notice an angel has floated down to see you.

She is carrying a key. Imagine you can take the key from her now. This key will unlock many of the things you have come here today to see.

Thank her and your special friend and imagine that they will both float away. Send them love as they gently float off into the distance. Take the key with you as we begin the next part of the adventure.

PAST LIVES

Now walk back toward the doorway and open the door. Walk back inside the beautiful room where we started.

Again, feel the great energy of this place as you look around. As you do, you notice there is an elevator at the other side of the room. Go ahead and walk over to it.

As you do, you will notice the buttons there. Go ahead and push the down button and notice the doors open. As they do, you see an angel is in there greeting you and welcoming you inside the elevator.

Go ahead and walk inside and as you look at the control panel, you will see we are on the 20th floor and we want to go all the way down to the ground floor. Push the ground floor button and start to go down.   With each floor you go down you will be twice as relaxed as you are on the previous floor and more relaxed than you have ever been before!

20-19-18-17-16-15- feel

yourself sinking into a deeper state of relaxation —14- so relaxed-13-12-11-10-9-8-7-more relaxed than you've ever been before - 6-5-4-3-2-1- and ground!

Now the elevator door opens and you step out into a hallway. Directly across from the elevator is a doorway. Open the door and look inside.

As you do, you realize you are looking inside a closet and in this closet are all of the clothes that you have ever worn before so it is totally familiar to you and feels very safe.

As you look inside, you notice an angel has come to meet you. Say hello and hand her the key you were given.

Remember also that you are still surrounded by a golden ball of light and that inside the ball of light, only that which is for your highest good can come through.

Take the angel by the hand and imagine the two of you could float back.....futher and further...back...into the closet.....go way, way, way back to a very early time that would be for your highest good. Go back to a time that would give you the most insight into yourself right now.

When you reach the appropriate spot, imagine that some clothes just light up and that the angel could hand them to you.

Now try them on and imagine that at the very end of the closet there is a mirror there. Now look in the mirror and notice what you see.

(If you cannot see any- thing, imagine the angel can tell you what you are wearing or you can have an inner knowing about it.)

What do your clothes look

*like? Look down and notice your
shoes. How do you feel?*

*Now imagine that the
mirror has a doorknob on it. I
want you to turn that doorknob
now and go out into your life!*

*Look around. What do
you see? Are you alone? Is there
anybody with you? If not,
imagine you can fast forward
now to a time when you are with
people and be there now.*

*As you look around at the
other people who are there with
you, is there anybody there who
you know in your current life -yes
or no?*

*If yes, imagine you can
have a higher understanding now
of that relationship and what the
two of you came to learn together.*

*Now imagine you can fast
forward to the very end of your
life. To the very last day of your
life. Remember you are still*

surrounded in a golden ball of light as you begin now to remember how it is that you die.

Now imagine yourself floating gently up, up up... to that special, peaceful place in between lives. Imagine now you can meet with your creator, however it is that you see that, and from here, you can have a higher perspective about your life.

What lessons were you to have learned in this lifetime?

How does that apply to things you are going through in your current life?

THE FUTURE

Now imagine an angel floats up to you and takes you by the hand and you begin now to float higher, higher and higher than you've ever been before.

Lifestream

Notice that you get so high you can see now you are floating over a line of light. This line looks like a beam of laser light.

Imagine this line represents your entire life as a soul. Imagine you are floating over it and you can now look into the future. As you do, notice how bright the future is.

In a moment, we are going to float out into the future to an unspecified time in the future. So go ahead now and begin to gently float with the angel out into the future.

If you have a tough decision to make about something right now, imagine you can float out and see a fork in the road.

Notice which path is lighter and float down that side to an unspecified time when you *are successfully completing your life's purpose.*

If you do not have a fork in the road, do the same. Just allow the angel to take you to sometime out in the future when you are successfully completing your life's purpose.

Float down into the event and see what is happening. How do you feel? Allow the angel to show you all the steps along the way that you took to be in this place now of successfully being all you can be.

Stay here a moment until you have full understanding about how you got here.

When you are ready, begin to float back toward now. When you are floating above now, imagine you can begin now to float down, down, down and find yourself coming through the ceiling of the beautiful room where we started.

Look around and notice this place. Thank the angel for bringing you back, and imagine she is floating away.

Now remember you are still surrounded by a golden ball of light and that only that which is of your highest good can come through.

Begin now to walk toward the door where you first came into the room. Open it and step out to the place where we started. Imagine your feet firmly planted on the ground.

Imagine a cord of brown light is going through the top of your head and traveling down your spine, down, down, down toward the floor and out the soles of your feet. The cord is going down, down, down, into the earth connecting you with the core of the earth.

Now in a moment, feeling totally grounded centered and balanced, you will come back into the room feeling totally rested and energized, as if you've had a full night's sleep. When I count back from 5 you will come back feeling better than ever. 5-4-3-feeling better than you ever have before -2-1- and you're back!!!

OVERVIEW

How did you enjoy that journey? The amazing thing is that we all have the power within us to truly tap into our own source and receive answers to all of the questions we ask!

I challenge you to repeat this process often. Each time you do, you will experience different insights into yourself through the past, present and future and the healing potential is unlimited!!

Conclusion

I give quite a few lectures, and recently I was out speaking to a group explaining my theories of the power of healing the heart.

A man in the back of the room raised his hand and asked, "Why do we have to do all of this?"

My answer: *you do not have to do anything!* I have found through my own grief recovery and with many of my clients that a spiritual journey of this kind is extraordinarily powerful!

It is like driving a car with a dirty windshield. Sometimes the greatest thing in the world may be right in front of you but you cannot see it until you clean the windows. Then you see it clearly and with a new appreciation.

Processes such as the ones explored in this book can help us let go of unproductive patterns that may be holding us back from reaching our highest potential, and can help us see the positive futures that are possible for each and every one of us.

Once again, I must restate what I said all along: past-lives may or may not be real. It really does not matter. In my opinion, they are real. Life is but an illusion anyway, so whatever lies in our subconscious is a real part of us, even if it

is outside of our conscious awareness. We create our own reality.

I like to believe that we
have lived before. We are a part of
some divine plan of perfection and
even what we perceive as our most
trying and bleakest moments are
serving a higher purpose as part of
the duality of the universe.

That is how we can move
toward a future where we can
create more positive experiences
through the only thing that really
exists in this world: **LOVE**.

Lifestream empowers us to
discover things about our souls and
use this information to better know
ourselves and the world around us.

When we are able to read
our own soul's records and have an
opportunity to sit and think about all
of the wonderful things we are as
spiritual beings, it makes us realize
that the only limitations we have are
those illusions we have created in
our minds.

There is something beyond the five senses that must be explored to gain higher understanding of ourselves and our world.

The vastness of the soul is like the ocean. All that it is, and all that it can be, lies unmanifest in the depths of the sea. Each hope and dream we have is out there waiting to be created, just like a wave is waiting to crash upon the shore.

Until it hits the shore, we will not know its size, nor its magnitude. We will not know how it will affect the world around us. It is something that remains a simple possibility until the moment it arrives.

Lifestream allows us to choose what kind of wave we want to make in the world.

Will it be the biggest and best we can be, or is our lesson in this lifetime to hold back? Neither is right or wrong, it is all about that which we came to learn.

Lifestream

To learn to love ourselves
and honor the path of our souls is
why we are all here. To live, to
love, to be...there is nothing more.
With that, I wish you a
Lifestream filled with love and joy.

Bibliography

Auerbach, Loyd. *ESP, Hauntings, and Poltergeists: A Parapsychologist's Handbook*. New York, NY: Warner Books, Inc., 1986.

Blackburn, Gabriele. *The Science and Art of the Pendulum: A Complete Course in Radiesthesia*. Ojai, CA: Idylwild Books, 1983.

Braden, Gregg. *The Isaiah Effect*. New York, NY: Random House, Inc. 2000.

Braden, Gregg. *The Lost Mode of Prayer*. Boulder, CO: Sounds True, 1999.

Chopra, Deepak. *Quantum Healing: Exploring the Frontiers* *of Mind/Body Medicine.* New York, NY: Bantam Books, 1989.

Chopra, Deepak. *The Seven Spiritual Laws of Success.* San Rafael, CA: Amber-Allen Publishing, 1993.

Choquette, Sonja. *Psychic Pathways.* New York: NY: Three Rivers Press, 1994.

Furst, Jeffrey. *Edgar Cayce's Story of Jesus.* New York, NY: Coward-McCann, Inc., 1968.

Gordon, Richard. *Quantum-Touch: The Power to Heal.* North Atlantic Books: Berkeley, CA, 1999.

Moody, Raymond A. *Life After Life.* San Francisco, CA: Harper Collins, 1975.

Moody, Raymond A. *Life After Loss.* San Francisco, CA: Harper Collins, 2001.

Moody, Raymond A. *The Light Beyond.* New York, NY: Bantam Books, 1988.

Myss, Carolyn. *Anatomy of the Spirit*. New York: NY: Three Rivers Press, 1996.

Myss Carolyn. *Sacred Contracts*. New York: NY: Harmony Books, 2001.

Rand, William Lee. *Reiki: The Healing Touch*. Southfield, MI: Vision Publications, 1998.

S

chiegl, Heinz. *Healing Magnetism*. York Beach, Maine: Samuel Weiser, Inc., 1987.

Sherwood, Keith. *Chakra Therapy*. St. Paul, MN: Llewellyn Publications, 1988.

Slate, Joe, Ph.D. *Psychic Vampires*. St. Paul, MN: Llewellyn Publications, 2002.

Stein, Diane. *Essential Reiki*. Freedom, CA: The Crossing Press, Inc. 1995.

Wauters, Ambika. *Chakras and Their Archetypes: Uniting Energy Awareness and Spiritual Growth*. Freedom, CA: The Crossing

Press, 1997.

Weiss, Brian. *Many Lives, Many Masters*. New York, NY: Simon & Schuster, 1988.